How to Speak
Religious Science

HOW
to SPEAK
RELIGIOUS
SCIENCE

DENNIS MERRITT JONES, R.SC. D.

 DeVorss Publicatons

How to Speak Religious Science

©1999 Dennis Merritt Jones
ISBN: 0-87516-727-6

Library of Congress Catalog Card Number 99-76344

DeVorss & Company, Publishers
P. O. Box 550
Marina del Rey CA 90294-0550

Printed in the United States of America

THE PURPOSE OF
THIS BOOK

The world is tired of mysteries, does not understand symbols, and longs for Reality.

> What is Reality?
> Where may It be found?
> How may It be used?

These are some of the questions we should like to have answered.

— Dr. Ernest Holmes
Science of Mind Textbook

This book has been created to assist the person who is on the pathway of Self-discovery in revealing the answer to the above questions.

WHO WE ARE

We are not Scientology.
We are not Christian Science.
We Are Religious Science.

Religious Science was founded in 1927 by Dr. Ernest Holmes. The teachings are called Science of Mind.

Religious Science exists to facilitate the reawakening of each individual's awareness of the higher Self.

Each Church of Religious Science, through Sunday services, Science of Mind classes, self-growth seminars, and individual counseling, provides an educational and spiritual process in a supportive environment, enabling all who desire to discover and know the ultimate Oneness of Universal Life to do so.

Religious Science is not in opposition to any religious belief or philosophy. Rather, it seeks to bring to light the thread of Truth that exists in all religions.

We recognize that each individual is on a path to his own fulfillment and must be guided by his own inner voice.* We offer practical and definite methods with which each individual can create positive life changes. Among the benefits of the teachings of Religious Science is the understanding of positive prayer or spiritual mind healing. We refer to this as Spiritual Mind Treatment.

In summary, Religious Science offers healing, spiritual understanding, and an opportunity to experience greater love, greater joy, and greater life expression. In the words of Dr. Ernest Holmes, *"There is a power for good in the universe, greater than you are, and you can use it!"*

*Use of the masculine pronoun is intended to be generic, encompassing all humankind.

■

DIVINE TRUTH
NEVER NEEDS TO BE SOLD,
JUST TOLD!

■

LISTED ON THE FOLLOWING PAGES
are many of the words that most often come up
while discussing what we believe with those people
who may be of a different religious persuasion.

The definitions are offered only as tools to better
help explain the Science of Mind and enhance one's
ability to communicate with others. Communication
is the key to all relationships.

Our goal in discussing our beliefs with others is
not to convert or save anyone, nor is it to prove who
is right and who is wrong. Our goal is to inform and
educate. The Infinite Intelligence within each person
will know if it's right for him.

A B S O L U T E

Is "Absolute" another word for God? Yes.

The absolute Truth is: God Is All There Is. As
Absolute Being, God is Infinite, Perfect, Unlimited,
Unconditioned, Self-Existent, and all
Self-Sufficient. (*See Reality*)

B I B L E

Do we use it? Of course.
Do we take it literally? No.

The Bible was written 2,000 to 3,000 years ago, by the Semitic people, for the Semitic people. The Bible is a valuable and valid source of Truth when read and understood according to the authors' consciousness and heritage. Truth is Truth, and the Bible must be read with an open mind, looking for the higher meaning in the stories, metaphors, and parables. To fully understand the Bible, one must understand idioms and the psychology used by the men who wrote the book. Yes, God did write the Bible, through the consciousness of human beings; therefore, we must understand humankind to understand the book.

CAUSE AND EFFECT

What is the difference between Cause and Effect?

Cause is always that which produces an effect. Metaphysically, we are always becoming cause to our effect by our thinking and deepest beliefs (see *Consciousness*). Our conscious mind is that point where cause begins. The effect or result is reflected in our physical bodies and the body of our affairs. When we become aware of this process, we find that as we change the cause (our thinking), the effect (our lives) changes automatically. As Religious Scientists, we deal in cause rather than effect. (See *Thought*)

CHRIST

Was Jesus the Christ? Yes

It's important to understand that Christ was not Jesus' last name; it is a title which acknowledges the fact that he fully understood and demonstrated his divine nature.

The word "Christ" comes from the Greek word *Christos*, which means "anointed" or "enlightened one." Christ is a universal idea, and each one "puts on the Christ" to the degree that he surrenders a limited sense of life to the divine realization of wholeness and unity with Good, Spirit—God.

CHRISTIAN

Do we consider ourselves Christians?

A "Christian" by definition is one who:
1. Believes in Jesus Christ
2. Follows his teachings

In the traditional sense, we do not consider ourselves Christian because we do not claim the man Jesus as our "Lord and Savior" (see *Savior*). However, we do believe in his teaching. The *Science of Mind* textbook is based largely upon his teachings.

We believe that the teacher Jesus came to show us each the way of the Christ (see *Christ*). Therefore, it is up to each individual to analyze his own life to decide if he is Christian or not. The message of the Christ is Unconditional Love, Nonjudgment, Forgiveness, Brotherhood, and Peace. Perhaps true Christianity is more of a lifestyle than it is any one particular religion.

CONSCIOUSNESS

What and where is consciousness?

Our consciousness is our mental awareness. It is both the conscious and the subconscious mind and all they contain. In essence, our consciousness is simply the sum total of everything we have ever believed and accepted to be the Truth about ourselves from the moment we were born until this moment in time.

Our consciousness is how we make individual use of Universal Mind. Our consciousness forms a belief system into which Life pours Itself (see *Mind*). We can change our consciousness through Spiritual Mind Treatment (see *Prayer*). The ultimate consciousness we want to develop would embrace an awareness that "God Is All There Is."

CULT

Are we a cult?

According to the dictionary, a cult is a group which studies a system of religious worship in admiration of, or devotion to, a person or thing.

In Religious Science we worship no one or no thing. To do so would be idolatry. We feel we need no "middle man" to intercede between ourselves and God. Unlike some teachings that have begun to worship the messenger instead of the message, Religious Science is the furthest thing from being a cult. Our teaching is universal, "in the open," and places no one above or below ourselves. We believe God is available to one and all equally.

DEATH

Do we believe in death? Yes—and no.

The divine principle of Life is an eternally unfolding, upward-spiraling movement. The spirit of God is the spirit of man, and it is both birthless and deathless. The principle of life cannot know death.

The human experience of dying is but the laying off of an old garment and the donning of a new one. There is a material body and spiritual body. This spiritual body is the so-called resurrection body.

DEMONSTRATION

We demonstrate at the level of our
ability to know the Truth.

A demonstration is simply the *result* of our mental
and spiritual work, which creates a greater and more
abundant life. Our demonstrations may be large or
small. We should celebrate them all because they
illustrate our ability to consciously know the *Truth*
and use Principle in positive ways! (See *Principle* and
Truth)

D E S T I N Y

Do we believe in predestination?

The only destiny that *we* have we decree by what we
think and embody today, becoming our reality
tomorrow. Our destiny is simply the perfect outpic-
turing of our individualized use of the Law of Cause
and Effect. (See *Cause and Effect* and *Consciousness*)

EVIL

Do we believe in a devil? No.

To believe in a devil would be to believe in duality or, in other words, to believe that there could be God— and some opposing power. There is not a power for good and a power for evil; there is only one power, and it is God. There are people, however, who misuse their power. The only devil we shall ever know is that which appears as a result of our own negative thinking, which then creates negative results. The devil is not a person, but an idea based in hellish thinking. (See *Hell*)

 22

DIAGNOSIS

Medically, a diagnosis is a recognition of the presence of disease, according to symptoms or conditions.

To Religious Scientists, a diagnosis is nothing more than an *opinion* about current conditions. We know that while conditions may be facts, facts can also change. A diagnosis should not be ignored, because God's intelligence *can* be revealed in and through medical opinions, however, it is not a verdict or a death sentence. We know that as we do our work in consciousness, we are operating at the Spiritual level. This means that we are reminding ourselves that God is First Cause to all our experience and that in the mind of God there is no disease, nor any other discordant condition. (See *Prayer*)

DISEASE

"Dis"-ease is simply an effect of wrong thinking.

It is an impersonal thought force operating through people which is not the truth about them. To the degree which our creative minds become "at-ease," dis-ease in our bodies will dis-appear. As we become more aware of the true presence of God at the very center of our being, inner peace will be the result. God-Self awareness is the key to being at-ease.

DOCTORS AND MEDICINE

Do we believe in the use of doctors and medicine?

We believe that God is omnipresent and therefore can do Its healing work in many ways. Certainly if God is everywhere, in everyone, then the intelligence of God can and does work through the doctor's mind and body as well as through any medication prescribed.

Of course, the ultimate goal for us as Religious Scientists is to understand that it is our thinking which creates all conditions in our bodies and the body of our affairs. It is a simple case of cause and effect. As we grow in our awareness of this truth, we know there will come a time when we are so fully aligned with the power and presence of God within us that there is no need for medical attention, for we are maintained in our natural state of perfection and wholeness. "Perfect God, perfect man, perfect being"!

D U A L I T Y

What is duality and how does it affect us?

Duality is the belief in two separate and opposing powers. We heal this fear by experiencing God's presence within us first, then realizing that God is always Omnipresent.

Duality results from a fear-based belief that we are, could, or might possibly be separate from God or Good; and the appearance of "things, conditions, and individuals" in the material world seems to reinforce this belief. (See *Omnipresent, Reality,* and *Devil*)

E M B O D Y

What is embodiment, and how do we use it?

To embody is to "give form or make part of." When we embody our thoughts and words through Spiritual Mind Treatment, we are actually allowing our thoughts to generate feelings. As our thought generates a feeling, we "give it form or make it part of" our entire being, spiritually, mentally, and physically.

Embodiment conveys to subconscious mind our acceptance of a conscious idea. We embody things constructively when we *believe* in what we *want* and want what we believe in. (See *Truth*)

E NERGY

Is "energy" another word for God? Yes!

Divine Energy is at the center and circumference of all that is. Quantum physics tells us energy is everywhere present and working even down to the subatomic level. Metaphysics tells us that energy in any form is God in action. All energy is creative. We direct energy first by understanding it and then by unifying *with it*. (See *Thought*)

E TERNAL

What does eternality mean to us as Religious Scientists?

The Eternal is the essence of God, which has no beginning and no end. It is without time or space. There is that part of each of us which is also eternal, because we are One in God. (See *Death* and *Reincarnation*)

E V I L

Evil is simply the word "devil"
without the letter "d."

Evil is an experience of the soul on its journey
toward the realization of Reality. (See *Reality*)

Of itself, evil is neither person, place, nor thing
and will disappear in exact proportion as we cease
thinking negatively and using destructive methods.
As long as we make mistakes we shall be automatically punished. A simple case of cause and effect.
(See *Sin*)

 E A R

What is fear, and how can we deal with it?

Metaphysically, fear is an emotional experience generated by a sense of separation from Source, God. All fear is attached to a concern of loss at some level. A full realization of God's Presence, as *source* and *supply* of *whatever* is needed to sustain us in wholeness, will neutralize fear. Fear is simply the lack of the awareness of God's Presence, which in Its highest vibration is love. (See *Love*)

G O D

Do we believe in God? Of course!
God is all we believe in.

God is the First Cause, the Great I Am, the One and Only. God is Spirit or Creative Energy, which is the cause of all visible things. God is all that we see and do not see.

God is Love, Wisdom, Intelligence, Power, Substance, and Mind. God is the Truth that is real, the Principle that is dependable.

To the degree that we can experience the presence of God in us, and as us, we shall be whole.

H E A V E N

Do we believe in a Heaven?

Heaven is an inner state of happiness. It is not a place or locality "out there" somewhere with streets paved in gold. It is a real state of being. The Kingdom of Heaven is within and can be fully experienced when we bond and unify with the presence of God at the center of our very being.

H E L L

Do we believe in a Hell?

Hell, just like Heaven, is a state of mind, all based
on our awareness or lack of awareness of the presence
of God within us.

Hell is a discordant state of being, a belief in
duality, a belief or sense of separation from Source,
God. Many people are filled with hellish thoughts
and therefore experience a "living hell" every day.

I AM

I Am That I Am!
The "I Am" is the highest name of God.

The "I Am" is both individual and universal. As we begin to walk in the "I Am" consciousness, we heal all sense of separation from God. God In Me As Me Is Me! Affirming "I Am" is the most powerful statement we can make. The impartial Law of Mind also affirms that what we place "I Am" in front of, we become.

IMMORTALITY

See Death

JESUS

Was Jesus the son of God? Yes.

We believe that Jesus was indeed the son of God—
and so is every other human being the son or daugh-
ter of God.

J UDGMENT

How does judgment affect us?

When the teacher Jesus said, "Judge not that you shall not be judged," he was simply referring to the Law of Cause and Effect. Since judgment is passed in our own mind, it impacts necessarily on our own experience, and not necessarily the experience of the person we are judging. When we judge others (or ourselves), we only create a sense of separation between ourselves and God.

It is also not ours to judge if others are deserving of some form of punishment. The Law of Cause and Effect operates without judgment. There is no punishment—only consequences. When we begin to see first and foremost the Presence of God in ourselves and others we have no need or desire to judge. (See *Sin*)

K A R M A

Do we believe in karma?

Karma is neither good nor bad, as it is not a thing in itself. It is simply the use we make of our mentality through the Law of Cause and Effect. Therefore, at any given moment we can begin to change our present as well as our future, because we can change our minds about the way we think and believe.

We do not recognize karma as inevitable retribution or reward, because God cannot hold judgments or grudges. As we learn from our mistakes and forgive ourselves, we let go of the past and all of its ties. This moment is our point of power and now is when we become cause to a new effect or new karma. (See *Destiny*)

L A W

The law is Mind in action.

The Law of Mind is the creative medium through which Spirit as Conscious Mind moves. The Law is deductive only. It receives the impress of thought and acts upon it much in the same way the creative medium of the earth's soil receives a seed, never rejecting it.

Whatever we think, believe in, feel, visualize, image, read, and talk about is going into the creative medium of our subconscious mind, which is our individualized use of Universal Mind. The Law is a blind force, and whatever goes into the subconscious state of our thought tends to return as some condition or effect. (See *Mind*)

L O V E

God is the essence of love.

"He that loveth not, knoweth not God; for God is Love" (1 John 4:8). Love is the self-givingness of spirit to its creation and is a cosmic force whose sweep is irresistible. Love is the highest vibration in the universe; nothing can withstand its embrace. The opposite of love is fear. In the light and vibration of love, the darkness of fear cannot exist. To know God's presence is to experience unconditional love. To see the presence of God in others is to love them. Unconditional love is always the answer.

MEDITATION

What is meditation, and how do we use it?

Meditation is simply quieting the conscious mind to facilitate a fuller experience of God's presence. Meditation is not for the purpose of praying or receiving answers. It is *after we meditate* that the higher Self may be revealed in the form of guidance or desired answers.

There are many forms of meditation, and one is not better than another. Meditation will help instill a deep sense of inner peace and relaxation, which benefits us spiritually, mentally, and physically.

METAPHYSICS

*Are we a metaphysical teaching
and what is metaphysics?*

Religious Science is a metaphysically based organization. There is nothing mysterious or supernatural about metaphysics. *Meta* means above or beyond, and *physical* means material or that which is experienced by the five senses. Metaphysics is simply the study of God as Creative Intelligence or Universal Mind, which is *everywhere* present, in and through all that we see, touch, smell, hear, taste. . . and beyond! (See *Omnipresent*)

M I N D

By "Mind" do we mean God's mind? Yes.

We also mean our own mind, as we are all one in God. There is actually no such thing as "your" mind and "my" mind, "his" mind or "her" mind, and God's mind. There is just one mind in which we all live, move, and have our being.

This mind is both conscious and subconscious. Conscious mind is the spirit either in God or man, and subconscious mind is the law of conscious mind in action and is, therefore, subject to conscious mind. Spirit moves through the law of mind to create (see *Cause* and *Effect*). That which we call "our mind" is simply that point in God-consciousness where we are aware of Self. (See *Spirit*)

N E W   A G E

Are we part of the New Age movement?
Do we believe in the use of crystals, channelers,
psychics, hypnotism or tarot cards and astrology?

Religious Science is in the New Thought Movement,
not the New Age Movement. While we are in a new
age of scientific discoveries and spiritual awakenings,
there is nothing new about the principles we study
and strive to apply in our daily lives. As *New
Thought,* Religious Science teaches the age-old wisdom of many of the world's great religions in a *new*
and contemporary format. This wisdom always leads
us back to the fact that our Truth and connection to
God can only be found within; therefore, we feel no

need to use any "tool" outside of our own consciousness to experience total wholeness, peace of mind, and a balanced life.

We do not feel the need to turn to aids or entities outside of our own innate intelligence for divine guidance or advice. To do so would be to give our power away. Religious Science and Science of Mind exist for one reason: "To help each person discover his own true inner power," not to take it away from him. God is the only true power. It is First Cause and must first be found within each individual, not in the outer world. Our desire is to heal any and all feeling of belief in separation from the source of all our good—God. This is an inner experience and an age-old Truth!

NEW THOUGHT

See *New Age*

O M N I P O T E N C E

The All-Powerful One God!

The benefit in knowing that God is all-powerful lies in the fact that we are One with this Power. As we begin to experience the presence of God within, we know we can let this power do wonderful things through us.

This is where our power in Spiritual Mind Treatment comes from. We know that we of ourselves do nothing but realize the Divine Truth. It is God within that does the work. (See *Truth*)

OMNIPRESENCE

The Constant Presence of the Universal Whole!
God Is All There Is!

There's not a spot where God is not! The entire
premise of Science of Mind rests solely on the fact
that "God Is All There Is"; the Alpha and the
Omega, the Beginning and the End, and everything
in-between.

While we know we are not all that God is, God is
all that we are. All discord in our lives arises because
at some level we have created a sense of separation
from God. Our ultimate goal in Science of Mind is
to heal this mistaken belief. As we daily practice our

unity with God by experiencing God's full presence at the center and circumference of our experience, a deep and fulfilling sense of Inner Peace and Wholeness will be the result. This is the Peace of God which truly does pass all understanding.

OMNISCIENCE

The All-Knowing Mind of God!

The Truth is there has never been nor will there ever be a problem or question the solution or answer to which doesn't already exist in the Omniscient Mind of God.

Through Spiritual Mind Treatment and meditation, we can consciously align with this Omniscient Mind of God, realizing that we already exist in It. As we do this, we begin to draw into our minds the wisdom and courage necessary to heal us in our difficulties.

We could begin daily to affirm and know: "God in me as me Is me, and therefore I *now know* what I need to know!"

PRACTITIONER

What is a practitioner?
When and why would I use one?

A practitioner is a person who is trained and licensed by Religious Science International or the United Church of Religious Science to perform Spiritual Mind Treatment for others (see *Prayer*). A practitioner does not counsel or give advice.

To do treatment work is to practice mental and spiritual healing, and to demonstrate for other than physical healing. All healing is done in consciousness and is reflected in the physical body and the body of one's affairs. Because the practitioner knows he and the person for whom he is treating are both one in

the Mind of God, he treats to know within *himself*
the truth *about* that person. Being one in
Mind, this self-knowingness rises into the consciousness of the one being treated. (See *Mind* and
Consciousness)

One might use the services of a licensed practitioner when one is emotionally entangled or too close
to a problem to consciously know the Spiritual Truth
about himself. (See *Truth*)

PRAYER

Do we pray in our teaching?

Prayer, by definition, means a "humble communication in thought or speech to God or to an object of worship expressing supplication, confession, and praise."

In Religious Science we do communicate in thought and speech with God through a process we call Spiritual Mind Treatment, or positive prayer. We believe that God has already given us, by our divine birthright, all that we ever will need to live a complete, healthy, whole, and prosperous life; our only job is to accept it! The communication always takes place within our own consciousness and mind.

Spiritual Mind Treatment is simply a process used to change our consciousness or belief system. Treatment acknowledges to Mind (or Law) that what we are treating for already exists and is ours. There is never any asking, begging, or supplication—only acceptance. The Law of Cause and Effect makes it so. Indeed, it is done unto us as we believe!

P R I N C I P L E

What is the Principle upon which
Science of Mind is based?

Science of Mind is the study of the Principle of
Being. Principle is defined as: "A fundamental Truth
or Law." We might say that because God Is All
There Is, Principle is the Intelligence of God in
action.

How does Principle operate? By means of each of
us, the Intelligence of God, as conscious mind,
moves through a field of subconscious mind (or creative medium), creating a result (or effect). Knowing
that we all exist in the One Mind of God, we each
individualize this Principle every time we think and

feel. As we understand Principle and how It operates, we can then choose to rely upon It to change our lives in positive ways. Principle is *not* bound by precedent! (See *Law*)

PUNISHMENT

See Sin

R ACE MIND

What is race mind and what does it do?

Also referred to as the collective unconscious or
social belief system, race mind is the collective
unconscious thought of the entire human race. It is
a thought force that permeates the entire planet.

Race mind suggestion is the human belief system
operating through the mentality of any individual
who is open and receptive to it. If we are not aware,
it is quite easy to slip into the vibration and influ-
ence of race mind. Race suggestion can be a prolific
source of negative energy resulting in disease.

We can rise above the negative vibration of race thought by consciously focusing our awareness daily upon a higher reality. Race mind cannot operate through one who is fully aware of God's presence in and around him.

R E A L I T Y

We live in a world where that which we can see,
touch, and smell seems like reality—
but it is actually our unreality!

The "Ultimate Reality" is the absolute truth, which
behind all form is the formless energy and intelligence of the one God. The apparent reality (that
which we see, touch, and smell) is just that—it
appears to be something, and it is always subject to
change. Ultimate Reality is changeless perfection;
therefore, the Real Self is perfection, for God could
not know anything unlike Itself. The spirit of God
within us and all around us is the only true reality.

As we begin to get in touch daily with this perfect principle, we can then demonstrate it in our daily lives. Perfect God, Perfect Man, Perfect Being—this is the Absolute Truth!

REALIZATION

*A realization is an impression of
Reality on the mind.*

The ultimate Reality is: God Is All There Is. As we
live and move and have our Being within this reality,
divine Realization will become commonplace for us.

A realization may be experienced as a divine
"Ah-ha!" It's simply an awareness of God's presence,
infused within us and around us in whatever we are
saying or doing. (See *Reality*)

R EINCARNATION

Do we believe in reincarnation?

On page 387 of the *Science of Mind* textbook, Dr. Ernest Holmes writes: *The spiral of life is upward. Evolution carries us forward, not backward. Eternal and progressive expansion is law and there are no breaks in continuity. . . . I can believe in planes beyond this one without number, in eternal progress. I cannot believe that nature is limited to one sphere of action.*

Life is an eternal flow, and we are streams of consciousness within this flow, forever unfolding. The question of reincarnation is meaningless when we accept the fact that at some level we have always been and shall always be; it's what we do today with who we are that matters. (See *Eternal* and *Destiny*)

R ELATIVE

*The relative is that which depends on
something else for its existence.*

In Religious Science, the relative is anything we
experience with the five senses of sight, hearing,
touch, taste, and smell. While the relative world may
appear as conditions separate and apart from the All,
it is not. God is all there is.

In the beginning, there was only God, who so
desired to be more fully expressed, that out of Itself
It created form through which to do so. Hence, the
relative. The relative is really another term for the
Body of God. God is Absolute and Relative! (See
Absolute and *Universe*)

RELIGION

*Any religion is simply the giving of a
certain form to humankind's idea of God.*

The word "religion" comes from the Greek/Latin
word *religare,* which means "to bind together."

It seems, however, that many of the world's religions have done just the opposite, separating
humankind not only from one another but from
God also. All religions could assist their members in
realizing their unity with one another and God. This
is what Religious Science teaches.

RELIGIOUS SCIENCE

Is Religious Science a religion?

The Church of Religious Science is the institution or organization that houses or gives form to the teaching called the Science of Mind.

In its broadest sense, Religious Science can be approached as a science, a philosophy *and* a religion. As a religion, Religious Science is a straightforward approach to the Universal Truths found in many of the world's great religions. The Principles we believe in free us from guilt, fear, and superstition. (See *Science of Mind*)

RESURRECTION

See Death

S AVIOR

Is Jesus our savior? No.

Jesus was a wayshower and master teacher who knew the divine Truth about himself and all others. We do not believe he died on a cross to save us from sin. (See *Sin*)

We look to the teacher Jesus as the great example rather than the great exception. In this teaching, no attempt is made to rob Jesus of his greatness or refute his teachings. If anything, Science of Mind is based on his teachings. "The works that I do shall you do also; and greater works than these you shall do." Therein lies the divine potential for all humankind.

 70

SCIENCE OF MIND

What is the Science of Mind?

The Science of Mind is the name of the book first written by Dr. Ernest Holmes in 1926 and revised by him in 1938. It became the text and basis for the teaching of Science of Mind as a science, philosophy, and religion for many thousands of people worldwide.

As a science, the Science of Mind is based on specific universal principles that many of the world's leading scientists are now proving. As a philosophy, the Science of Mind is a simple, practical, and down-to-earth way of understanding the full nature of the Universe and our relationship to it.

For the dedicated student, the Science of Mind is not just a teaching but a way of life! (See *Religious Science*)

S I N

Do we believe that man is a sinner?

The word "sin" comes from an ancient Greek term. When an archer missed his target with his arrow, he sinned. Sin means to miss the mark or to make a mistake.

There is no sin but a mistake, and no punishment but a consequence. The Law of Cause and Effect always brings with it the consequences of the action or mistake.

God does not punish sin. As we correct our mistakes, we "forgive our own sins." God does not sit in judgment. God is a God of love, not anger, judgment, or punishment. God allows us to answer for our own mistakes (sins) to the immutable Law of Cause and Effect. There is no good or bad—only consequences.

# S O U L

Do we believe that man has a soul? Yes.

The truth is there is only one Soul and it is the Soul of the Universe. Individual man's soul is simply that point within him where the Universe (or God) personalizes Itself.

We believe that the soul is man's creative medium and is therefore subjective (or subject) to his conscious thought. The soul is that perfect part of our being which accepts us and our actions, never judging us as right or wrong, always ready to "assist" us in achieving whatever we choose to do when we believe we can do it.

The soul has been referred to as the "mirror of mind," because it reflects the forms of thought which are given it. We choose the thoughts it reflects (or in other words, brings into an experience). (See *Law*)

S P I R I T

Does man have a spirit? Of course!

More than that, man actually *is* spirit. We believe that the Spirit of God desired to be more fully expressed, so out of Itself It created form to express through.

That form takes many different shapes and conditions. Among the highest forms of God's expression is the human form—You! We are each the Spirit of God individualized. Rather than trying as human beings to have a "spiritual experience," we should realize that we are truly spiritual beings having a human experience.

You are not just a body of flesh and bones! There is a self-conscious, free-choosing, volitional spirit at the center of your being. This Spirit is sometimes referred to as "the Inner Observer."

As we become more aware of the presence of the spirit that we really are, we automatically begin to live in the awareness that God and we are truly one. Spirit thinks consciously, and this thought moves through the creative, subjective medium of mind (our soul) and becomes objectified in our outer world of effect. Spirit is the cause; the result of the thought is the effect.

T H O U G H T

"Thought" is the movement of consciousness.

As Religious Scientists, we know that our thoughts
are energy being directed in a specific way.

Our thought originates as cause in our conscious
mind, which then moves through our subconscious
mind as Law. In other words, our thoughts work
through Law, but that Law is *consciously* set in
motion. (This is how thoughts become things.) The
realization that *we* are responsible for the thoughts
we think and thus can change them is the beginning
of our *using* Law *consciously!* Change your thinking,
change your life! (See *Law* and *Embody*)

TREATMENT

See Prayer

TRUTH

The Truth is that which is.

It is the Cause and Power in and through everything. It is birthless, deathless, changeless, complete, perfect, whole, self-existent, causeless, almighty, Spirit, Law, Mind, Intelligence, Reality—GOD.

When the teacher Jesus said, "Know the truth and the truth shall set you free," he was simply saying that to the degree you know the truth about yourself, you will be free and able to direct your own life in wonderful, creative, meaningful ways, simply by understanding that your every thought is creative.

The truth about you is, "God in you, as you, is you." God really is all that is. Know this truth and you are free to express your true Self!

U N I V E R S E

The Universe is simply the body of God.

It is that which it created out of itself in order to be more fully expressed. (See *Relative*)

Scientists tell us the Universe is continually expanding. This is the creative divine Urge of God always becoming more than it was yesterday. This same creative divine Urge permeates every cell in our bodies. It is that urge which causes us to grow and be more than we were yesterday. Our bodies are simply mini-universes—the microcosm within the macrocosm.

WORD OF GOD

The Word means the ability of Spirit
to declare itself into manifestation, into form.
The Word of God simply means the
Self-Contemplation of the Spirit.
"I Am that I Am."

The physical universe which we see, as well as the invisible Universe, which must also exist, constitute the Self-Contemplation of God.

This is meaningful to us because as incarnations of the One Spirit of God, each time we think or contemplate, we are really speaking the "word" into creative Mind, and, through the law of cause and effect, our "word" becomes manifest!

IN SUMMARY

Religious Science churches and the teaching of Science of Mind have one primary purpose: To assist the individual who desires and is willing to heal his life of any and all discord, fear, superstition, guilt, and sense of lack. Wholeness is a Reality, and it can be found at the very center of who and what we are now.

Our desire as an organization is not based so much on instructing willing individuals in *what* to think but rather in *how* to think. We can best learn how to think by first understanding that we live in a Spiritual Universe that operates on purpose, by responding to *our* thoughts, feelings, and deepest beliefs.

It is we, and we alone, who ultimately create our experience. While this Truth may at times be a challenge to accept, it is also the Truth which sets us free. As we learn to take responsibility for our thinking, we shall see our lives transformed in incredible and wonderful ways. We can begin to live, move, and have our being in a greater awareness that God really is *All* that is. As we honor Its Presence in all people and places (including ourselves, wherever we may be) the Divine Principle of Life automatically honors us.

In the conclusion of the *Science of Mind* textbook, Dr. Ernest Holmes summarized this all very well when he wrote:

The practice of Truth is personal to each, and in the long run no one can live our life for us. To each is given what he needs and the gifts of heaven come alike to all. How we shall use these gifts is all that matters!

In other words, there is a Power for good in the Universe, greater than you, and you *can* use it *now.*

This is God's gift to you—and what you decide to do *with it* is your gift to God!

DECLARATION of PRINCIPLES

We believe in God, the Living Spirit Almighty, one, indestructible, absolute and self-existent Cause.

We believe that this One manifests Itself in and through all creation, but is not absorbed by Its creation.

We Believe that the manifest universe is the body of God. It is the logical and necessary outcome of the infinite self-knowingness of God.

We believe in the incarnation of the Spirit in man and that all men are incarnations of the One Spirit.

We believe in the eternality, the immortality, and the continuity of the individual soul, forever and ever expanding.

We believe that the Kingdom of Heaven is within man and that we experience the Kingdom to the degree that we become conscious of It.

We believe the ultimate goal of life is a complete emancipation from all discord of every nature, and that this goal is sure to be attained by all.

We believe in the unity of all life, and that the highest God and the innermost God is one God.

We believe that God is personal to all who feel this Indwelling Presence.

We believe in the direct revelation of Truth through the intuitive and spiritual nature of man, and that any man may become a revealer of Truth who lives in close contact with the Indwelling God.

We believe that the Universal Spirit, which is God, operates through a Universal Mind, which is the Law of God, and that we are surrounded by this creative Mind, which receives the direct impress of our thought and acts upon it.

We believe in the healing of the sick through the power of this Mind.

We believe in the control of conditions through the power of this Mind.

We believe in the eternal Goodness, the eternal Loving-kindness, and the eternal Givingness of Life to all.

We believe in our own soul, our own spirit, and our own destiny, for we understand that the life of man is God.

—Ernest Holmes

For further information,

call your local Church of Religious Science,

or Religious Science International at:

(800)662-1348

1636 West First Avenue

Spokane, Washington 99204

e-mail RSIHO@aol.com